LYFE

Live Your Faith Every Day

Rachel Kirkpatrick

TATE PUBLISHING
AND ENTERPRISES, LLC

LYFE
Copyright © 2012 by Rachel Kirkpatrick. All rights reserved.

No part of this publication may be reproduced, stored in a retrieval system or transmitted in any way by any means, electronic, mechanical, photocopy, recording or otherwise without the prior permission of the author except as provided by USA copyright law.

Scriptures taken from the *Holy Bible, New International Version*®, NIV®. Copyright © 1973, 1978, 1984 by Biblica, Inc.™ Used by permission of Zondervan. All rights reserved worldwide. www.zondervan.com

This book is designed to provide accurate and authoritative information with regard to the subject matter covered. This information is given with the understanding that neither the author nor Tate Publishing, LLC is engaged in rendering legal, professional advice. Since the details of your situation are fact dependent, you should additionally seek the services of a competent professional.

The opinions expressed by the author are not necessarily those of Tate Publishing, LLC.

Published by Tate Publishing & Enterprises, LLC
127 E. Trade Center Terrace | Mustang, Oklahoma 73064 USA
1.888.361.9473 | www.tatepublishing.com

Tate Publishing is committed to excellence in the publishing industry. The company reflects the philosophy established by the founders, based on Psalm 68:11,
"The Lord gave the word and great was the company of those who published it."

Book design copyright © 2012 by Tate Publishing, LLC. All rights reserved.
Cover design by Joel Uber
Interior design by Chelsea Womble

Published in the United States of America

ISBN: 978-1-61862-858-9
1. Religion / Christian Life / Devotional
2. Religion / Biblical Stuies / General
12.05.10

A SPECIAL PRAYER AND DEDICATION

This book is for my mom, who is still unsure.

ACKNOWLEDGMENTS

A special thanks to:

God, who has saved my life in more ways than one.

Jason, who believed in me even when I didn't believe in myself.

Sarah, whose faith is unwavering and whose selflessness has been an inspiration to me since the day we met.

Powell Church, where I have found my spiritual home, seeking rejuvenation, fellowship, and accountability on a regular basis.

My LYFE Support ladies: Angelina, Anne, Beth, Kelly, Kim R., Kim S., Laura, Lee Ann, Lindsey, Lynda, Renee, Sarah, Theresa, without whom I wouldn't have had the encouragement to pursue this project.

PREFACE

Besides a wedding and a funeral, I had never stepped foot into a church until I went to a lock-in with my friend when I was in the seventh grade. Thank goodness for Young Life, where I spent many Thursday evenings singing songs and spending time with my faithful peers. My freshman year at Windy Gap, North Carolina, I was sitting on a large embankment on a cool November night, all alone praying and pondering about my faith. After seeing two shooting stars and shedding some tears, I asked Jesus to be my Savior.

Easy enough, right? Except I had to go back to school, be around all my friends, and try to balance the pressure to fit in with my newfound faith. Long story short, I failed over and over again. I would love to say that I was just experimenting, but the truth is that I experimented frequently and self-destructively.

I would, however, with God's intervention, go through periods where I would isolate myself and walk the straight and narrow for months at a time. This is the cycle I lived in until after I finished graduate school.

There have been several moments that helped me reconnect with God and rekindle our relationship. There was one God-sized nudge that reminded me that the distance between us had gotten unbearably large. More precisely, the chasm I'd created was so gaping that I could barely recognize that teenage girl who had promised her heart and life to God on that brisk November night so many years before.

One spring evening, after what had become a fairly routine night of partying, I was driving home. I am ashamed that I would drink and drive, but after lots of prayer and pain, I have asked God for forgiveness, and I have forgiven myself. Using back roads is always the faulty logic of the inebriated. I was on roads I did not know, trying—without much success—to follow my friend. Because of the overgrown brush, I did not see the stop sign or realize it was a T-intersection. A split second later, I slammed on my breaks and skidded through the intersection at about thirty-five miles per hour. Although it was in the flash of an instant, I still remember the paralyzing fear I felt in the pit of my stomach, the smell of the airbag dust in the air, and the sensation of being completely helpless. In less than two seconds, my cell phone had flown from the console, my glasses were knocked from my face, and my car was practically vertical in the bottom of a twelve-foot ditch. It was nearly midnight, and I was stranded in the middle of nowhere. Thankfully, I was not injured, but the car was totaled.

I climbed out of my car, and the door nearly flew off its hinges when I opened it because the embankment was so steep. I managed to scale the hill and had to wait for someone to drive by and see me. Without streetlights to stand under , I had no choice but to loiter in the middle of the road and wait for help. I was alone, petrified, and clueless. I'm not sure how long it took for someone to come by, but eventually the police showed up. I did all the field sobriety tests (of course thinking that I was doing an outstanding job), and then they promptly hauled me to the slammer.

As you know from watching TV, you get one phone call from jail. There was one small problem—nix that, two small problems. One, I was intoxicated. Two, I didn't know my parents' long distance number by heart. They took my prints and my mug shot. If I were ever to run for public office, I'm sure these would make the front page. I eventually called my parents collect. They woke up at two o'clock in the morning to four dreadful words: "Mom, I'm in jail." Believe it or not, they actually still love me. After donating my Corn Pops to the meth addict whom I was sharing the cell with, I was bailed out by the compassionate bondsman who also gave me a ride home. They won't let you leave jail unless you have a ride. My parents spent a ton of money on my legal fees. Thanks to a great lawyer, a previously untainted record, and an overcrowded penal system, I was sentenced to 120 hours of community service. Due to some tedious legal work, there is no official record of this nightmarish evening in my file.

There are only a handful of days that have changed the course of my future. The day I graduated from college, my wedding day, and the day our son was born are the first three that come to mind. But this incident changed the course of my life and my faith forever. Ironically enough, it was the accident that saved my life. I have come to be very thankful for the day that I totaled my car and landed in jail. I could have been killed, but God spared me. He saved me so that I could share the hope of redemption with others. Not everyone falls so far or so hard, but we all have struggles in our faith walk. My accident was my wake-up call. It helped me realize that the life I was leading was really leading me nowhere. And, no matter how many parties I went to or how many substances I consumed, I would never fill the God-sized void in my heart. There was only one thing left to do: ask God to clean up the mess I called "me."

I have spent the last ten years seeking to grow my relationship with God. Although, to be honest, it wasn't until the last three years that I have really learned to be comfortable enough with my faith to share it with others. In November of 2008, I was baptized and became a member at Powell Church. On that Sunday morning, I knew I was living the first day of the rest of my life.

I tell you my story so that you know I am not Mother Teresa. My past, and undoubtedly my future, is riddled with mistakes. Instead of focusing on the person I was, I have chosen to focus on the person God wants me to be. Every day is a new day to make a difference.

Fast forward to the present. God has moved me. I am typically a person who is eager to help others but completely uncomfortable with the idea of offering unsolicited help. After praying about it, God showed me that I don't have to wait to be asked. Since I long to be more Christlike, I was compelled to take action. Over the course of seven weeks, I made a decision to put Jesus at the helm of my day, every day. Like many people, my daily routine usually consisted of work, family, errands, household chores, and maybe a little television before my exhaustion-induced bedtime. With the exception of my morning devotional, Sundays, and maybe a few Wednesdays a month, Jesus was rarely present on my daily to-do list.

Over the course of writing and participating in this study, I reprioritized my daily routine. I intentionally invited Jesus to help me make my to-do list. I still went to work, spent time with my family, and took care of all my daily responsibilities, but I let Jesus be my guide. Instead of defining my days by what I accomplished, my days were defined by what He accomplished through me. He showed me how to love my family more deeply, sacrifice more of my time and energy to show concern for others, and that my relationship with Him is at its best when He's in charge. Hopefully, my experience will inspire others to rethink how they put their faith into action. Please walk with me and pray that all those who participate in this study find a greater love for mission, a greater appreciation for Jesus's life, and greater sense of obligation to their community.

Should you join me on this journey, these next seven weeks will be filled with devotion to prayer, the Word, and the called action to Christ's mission. Specifically, you will have a Jesus-centered task to complete every day for the next 49 days. It will include activities such as writing a letter, reaching out to a neighbor, donating to a charity, and living only a fraction of the sacrificial life that Jesus has called us to lead. At a minimum, you'll need twenty minutes per day to devote to this journey. It won't be easy, but I promise it will be worthwhile. It will require sacrificing some of your (not so) free time, but you may just get a glimpse at selfless devotion made by Jesus as he showed us The Way.

Therefore I urge you brothers, in view of God's mercy, to offer your bodies as living sacrifices, holy and pleasing to God—this is your spiritual act of worship. Do not conform any longer to the pattern of this world, but be transformed by the renewing of your mind. Then you will be able to test and approve what God's will is—his good, pleasing and perfect will.

Romans 12:1-2

WEEK 1: GROWING FROM THE INSIDE OUT

In order to prepare for this journey, you must prepare yourself. Your heart and mind must be spiritually open to the possibilities and ready for the sacrifices, so that your good works will take root and multiply. As a teacher, I often tell my students that they will only get out of the class what they put into it. If you give up your time, energy, resources, and even your self-awareness or insecurities, you will find that it is really more of a spiritual investment than a sacrifice. But if you're like me, sometimes all He gets is a few minutes of prayer before I nod off to sleep. God is amazing, but that's really a very narrow window of opportunity for Him to work in our lives. But what if we gave Him more? I love my comfort zone, and I often cling to it with white knuckles. Through this experience, I have learned that Jesus will take up residence in me wherever there is room. The hard part is leaving enough space for Him on a daily basis. But, by seeking Him, all of a sudden the ordinary, routine daily life has extraordinary promise. His presence exudes love and ensures a peace that only He can give. In short, Jesus has become my new comfort zone.

"Still other seed fell on good soil, where it produced a crop—a hundred, sixty or thirty times what was sown" (Matthew 13:8).

DAY 1: LET'S GET PERSONAL

Please answer all of the following questions as honestly as you can.

1. Besides Jesus, who do you admire the most and why?
   My husband, shows me how to see two sides to every story, makes me a better person. And my mom has the purest heart & always gives anyone the shirt off her back

2. What is your favorite part about being a Christian?
   Sharing it with others and trying to be an influence on my family.

3. What is your least favorite part about being a Christian?
   Being held accountable

4. Jesus sacrificed everything so that we may live. What is the hardest thing for you to give up in order for you to be more obedient to Him?

   Managing time for myself & for him.

5. List at least three things you hope to get out of this study.

   † *To be more christ like*
   † *To live through him 7 days a week*
   † *To show others my faith.*

DAY 2: SHOUT IT LOUD!

Today, you have three simple tasks.

1. You need to tell at least three people (who are not already doing this study) about your plans over the next several weeks. You can even invite them to join you if you think they'd be up for the challenge. Once you have proclaimed your intentions out loud, it is much more likely that you will follow through. Also, you will have a support group to offer an ear or lend a hand if a future task requires. Using the blanks provided, write down the names of the three people you've told.

   Brooke, mom, Kelsey, step-mom, Billie

2. You need to start saving your spare cash. On week six, you'll be giving a gift. You should try to save as much as you can. This may mean packing your lunch for the next several weeks, foregoing that special delicious treat, or finding creative ways to use the food already in the cupboard. There is not

a specific amount to save, but your gift should represent a personal sacrifice. In the blank provided, write down how much you intend to donate.

$ _30_

3. Read the following verse at least three times. First, read the verse out loud, even if it makes you feel a little crazy to be reading aloud to yourself. After the second reading, write down the words that stand out to you. After the final read through, write what it means to you to offer your body as a living sacrifice to God.

    "Therefore, I urge you, brothers, in view of God's mercy, to offer your bodies as living sacrifices, holy and pleasing to God—this is your spiritual act of worship" (Romans 12:1).

What does this verse mean to you?

Giving yourself to God, not just that one hour a week, but our whole selves.

DAY 3: DIVING INTO THE SCRIPTURE

I have heard it said that Scripture is like a love letter from home. If we really want to know what God wants for us and from us, all we have to do is read His Word.

Today, you need to set aside time to read James 1:14-26.

1. What is the most compelling verse or line from this section and why?
   Quick to listen, slow to speak, slow to be angry. I am always so quick to assume or judge or even talk

2. I am often worried about what others think of me and therefore tempted to allow my insecurities to paralyze me. Yet, seeking affirmation in anything or anyone besides my Father shows a complete

absence of faith. What are some of your greatest temptations and how do they impede your faith walk?

Being around other people who don't portray they are walking by faith, & I hang out w/ them & they probably think the same?

DAY 4: A RIPPLE IN THE POND

I still remember my chemistry teacher from twelve years ago. I don't know a lick of chemistry, but I will never forget the teacher. For Christmas my sophomore year, she gave us all a gift. She went around to each individual student and complimented us. Some students she imagined as famous artists or athletes. For me, the gangly, awkward, and insecure teenage girl, she said that I should be a super model. Ms. Smith could have been work-weary or stressed about the holidays, which would be totally understandable. But, she was willing to give us the gift of confidence instead. If busyness or exhaustion were valid excuses to forego our calling, we'd all be excused. We all know that Jesus was busy, and he never complained or made excuses. He obeyed His Father in spite of the cost. Thank the Lord for that!

On a very basic level, we all have the same needs: food, air, water, shelter, clothing, and love. What better way to share Jesus's love than to take a moment and let someone know that you noticed them and that they matter? Today you have the chance to share a gift, and it won't cost you a thing. Please try to complete each of these tasks from this day forward. You have no idea how far your ripple may go.

1. Smile when you enter a room, even if you're not having the best day.

2. Genuinely compliment at least two people.

3. Smile at a stranger.

4. Can you think of any other seemingly small gestures that may have a huge impact?
   Opening the door, ask how someone is doing

DAY 5: MAKE IT YOUR OWN

Today we will revisit the verse you read on Day 2.

> "Therefore, I urge you, brothers, in view of God's mercy, to offer your bodies as living sacrifices, holy and pleasing to God—this is your spiritual act of worship" (Romans 12:1).

1. Rewrite this verse in your own words.

   Everyone needs to listen, for God who brought us everything, give yourselves to him, obey him, this is how your soul will be complete through his holy word.

2. What does sacrifice mean to you?

   To give up something for something greater in hopes to come

3. What is the greatest sacrifice you've ever witnessed?

motherhood, policeman, firefighters, military, etc.

4. What is the greatest sacrifice you've ever made?

my money, myself, my things, my time for my family

DAY 6: SPENDING TIME WITH GOD

> Do not be anxious about anything, but in everything, by prayer and petition, with thanksgiving, present your request to God. And the peace of God, which transcends all understanding, will guard your hearts and your minds in Christ Jesus.
>
> Philippians 4:6-7

Today you will write a letter to God. It is your petition for forgiveness and peace. It is an opportunity to be gracious for His abundant love and mercy. In your letter, write down at least three things that happened this week for which you are thankful. God was with you all week and by thanking Him, you're acknowledging His presence in your life. Tell Him what you sacrificed, what you struggled with, and how you fell short. The best part of all is that He loves to hear from you and can always read your handwriting. I promise, He will never correct your grammar, punctuation or spelling.

You may use the space below to write your letter.

① First, I am thankful for my daughter. God has truly blessed me w/ a healthy

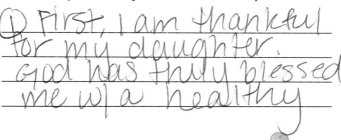

baby. second my husband, he helps me around the house + other areas, but he mainly helps me emotionally + spiritually. For that I am thankful. Third, all my parents being wonderful grandparents, they help so much w/ the baby and I am so thankful for all their help

DAY 7: A WEEK IN REVIEW

Let us take a moment and reflect on our first week.

1. Which day did you enjoy the most? Explain.

The first because it puts everything into perspective, who inspires us, what we love about faith + admitting what we're scared of. Puts the study in perspective of what we are about to dive into, + to be prepared to expand your faith.

2. Which task was the hardest for you to complete? Explain.

Probably re-writing the scripture in my own words, it takes me a while to understand what the reading was about, then it's tough to put into words.

3. Which task do you think made the most difference? Explain.

day 6 because it made me remember how blessed I am + how God has given me more than I deserve.

WEEK 2:
PUTTING FAMILY FIRST

A happy family is but an earlier heaven.

George Bernard Shaw

This week you are encouraged to make sure your family is ready to sacrifice valuable time with you over the next few weeks. It's not like you're moving out, but you will be sharing your time and energy with others. In order to make this a sustainable undertaking, you will need their support. Over the next six days, you will show them that they are loved and appreciated. Hopefully this week will feel more like a joy than a task. Keep these verses in mind throughout the week:

> "I tell you the truth," Jesus replied, "no one who has left home or brothers or sisters or mother or father or children or fields for me and the gospel will fail to receive a hundred times as much in this present age (homes, brothers, sisters, mothers, children and fields—and with them, persecutions) and in the age to come, eternal life."
>
> Mark 10:29-31

DAY 1: TURNING OFF AND TUNING IN

Today you get to make time for your immediate family. The only requirement is that you spend time together without interruption. Specifically, turn off your cell phones, iPods, laptops, televisions, stereos… While you are silently (hopefully not awkwardly) looking at one another, these are some of the topics you should consider discussing:

1. Please tell them about your study and what you're going to be doing over the next several weeks. See if they might want to help.

   I told my husband right before this bible study. He is praying that I get a lot out of it.

2. Ask them about the funniest thing that happened to them this week.

   Went and saw the movie Campaign!

3. Tell each of your family members three qualities that you love the most about them.

① great listener, great advice ② never argue, is so quick to see my side & always understands ③ is always touching me

4. Make plans to do something as a family before the end of this week.

Make plans to sit down & read Coraline's first book as a family.

DAY 2: THEIR BIGGEST FAN!

Today, read this very short story about love and compassion from *The Power of Intention* by Dr. Wayne W. Dyer (Dyer 2010).

> In Brooklyn, New York, Chush is a school that caters to learning-disabled children. At a Chush fundraising dinner, the father of a Chush child delivered an unforgettable speech. After extolling the school and its dedicated staff, he cried out, "Where is the perfection in my son Shaya? Everything God does is done with perfection. But my child cannot understand things as other children do."
>
> "I believe that when God brings a child like this into the world, the perfection that he seeks is in the way people react to this child." He then told the following story about his son Shaya.
>
> One afternoon Shaya and his father walked past a park where some boys were playing baseball. Shaya asked, "Do you think they will let me play?" Shaya's father knew that most boys would not want him on their team. But Shaya's father understood that if his son was chosen to play it would give him a sense of belonging. Shaya's father asked one of the boys

in the field if Shaya could play. The boy said, "We are losing by six runs, and it's the eighth inning. I guess he can be on our team and we'll try to put him up to bat in the ninth inning."

Shaya's father was ecstatic as Shaya smiled broadly. Shaya put on a glove and ran out into the field. In the bottom of the eighth inning, Shaya's team scored a few runs but was still behind by three. In the bottom of the ninth inning, Shaya's team scored again and now with two outs and the bases loaded, Shaya was scheduled to be up. Would the team actually let Shaya bat at this juncture and give away their chance to win the game?

Surprisingly, Shaya was given the bat. Everyone knew that it was all but impossible because Shaya didn't even know how to hold the bat properly. However, as Shaya stepped up to the plate, the pitcher moved a few steps to lob the ball in softly so Shaya should at least be able to make contact. The first pitch came in and Shaya swung clumsily and missed. One of Shaya's teammates came up to Shaya and together they held the bat waiting for the next pitch. The pitcher again took a few steps forward to toss the ball softly toward Shaya. As the pitch came in, Shaya and his teammate swung the bat and together they hit a slow ground ball to the pitcher. The pitcher picked up the soft grounder and threw it to right field. Everyone started yelling, "Shaya, run to first. Run to first." Never in his life had Shaya run to first. He scampered down the baseline wide-eyed and startled. By the time he reached first base, the right fielder had the ball.

The right-fielder threw the ball high and far over the third baseman's head. Everyone yelled, "Run to second, run to second." Shaya ran towards second base as the runners ahead of him deliriously circled the bases towards home. As Shaya reached second base, the opposing shortstop ran to him, turned him in the direction of third base and shouted, "Run to third." As Shaya rounded third, the boys from both teams ran behind him screaming, "Shaya run home." Shaya ran home, stepped on home plate and all 18 boys lifted him on their shoulders and made him the hero, as he had just hit a "grand slam" and won the game for his team.

"That day," said the father softly with tears now rolling down his face, "those 18 boys reached their level of God's perfection."

1. List all of the winners from this story and describe what they won.

The father, for always being patient + trying w/his son. Shaya for always having child-like faith. All 18 boys for recognizing the importance of another child's life since they have the ability to play ball + Shaya doesn't.

2. What is one lesson from this inspirational story that you can apply to your own life/family?

To try + see or find God's perfection bc sometimes it may be hard to see.

3. Do you have an inspirational family story to share?

My dad had GBS, I have never prayed so hard for him to stay alive, + by God's grace he ended up having a full recovery.

DAY 3:
MAKING YOUR SPECIAL SOMEONE FEEL LIKE SOMEONE SPECIAL

Today your extra time and energy should be devoted to the person you love the most. It could be a spouse, a parent, a love interest, or a best friend. It is the very first step in truly practicing selflessness. Do your very best to complete all of the following tasks today or over the course of the rest of this week. The greater challenge is remembering not to expect *anything* in return.

1. At some point during the day, drop them a line or note that tells them you're thinking of them and, if applicable, make sure they know you will be taking care of dinner tonight.

   I told my husband that he means the world to me!

2. If you can cook, make them their favorite dish. If you can't cook, take them to their favorite restaurant. If you can't afford a lavish meal, treat them to their favorite dessert.

   We cooked for the grandparents!

3. Find a way to make their life easier today. This could mean doing a chore that is normally theirs (i.e., household duties, washing car, picking up kids, errands, etc.).

   I cleaned the house and picked his stuff up! Let him sleep in!

4. Make sure that you thank them and let them know that you don't expect anything in return except their continued love and support as you work through this study.

he said ok!

5. Find one more personalized way to make your special someone feel like someone special.

I told him I admired him + it meant so much to him that I said that

DAY 4: GO, GO, GADGET ARMS!

Today you're sending a long-distance hug. You need to send at least one letter to a member in your family telling them how much you love them and why they are so special. You may send as many letters as you'd like, but please handwrite them and send them via snail mail. This may seem tedious, but everyone loves getting something in the mailbox besides bills. Not to mention, they will appreciate having a personalized reminder that they are important.

1. To whom did you write the letter(s)?

   Kelsey

2. Is there a reason why you chose this particular person or people?

   She doesn't get appreciated enough

3. Before today, when was the last time you wrote someone a letter?

   Baby shower, thank you notes!

4. When was the last time you received a letter, and how did it make you feel?

   Annie from work, it made me feel great! I love getting them!

DAY 5: FAMILY TIES

Take a look at each of the following verses about family and relationships and briefly summarize them in your own words.

Matthew 12:48-50
Everyone who obey's God + lives by him is "family"

Genesis 29:18-20
How love is worth the wait when you passionately love eachother!

Exodus 20:12
Obey your parents, they are your guide

Psalm 127:3
Children are a reward

1. Which of these verses is the most meaningful to you?
   Genesis, reminds me of Brent + I

2. Is there a family member for whom you are especially concerned?
   My little sister w/ Exodus

3. Who in your family has been your greatest role model and why?

   My mom because she has the biggest heart + will do anything for anyone.

4. Do you have a family member you could strengthen your relationship with?

   Yes, my husband + I can always grow in faith together.

5. Does Jesus's definition of family change the way you look at those you call your "family"?

   Yes, because I judge others sometimes + it's hard for me to treat them the same.

DAY 6: SPENDING TIME WITH YOUR FATHER

"Let the wise listen and add to their learning, and let the discerning get guidance" (Proverbs 1:5).

Today, set aside at least twenty minutes to spend in complete silence. Turn off all distractions (cell phone, television, radio) and find a quiet haven where you can really focus on hearing His voice. You might be surprised by how much He has to say when your heart is focused on Him. Please remember to ask God for spiritual guidance as you begin to juggle your family life with the demands of this study. What is He revealing about your relationships?

In the space below, write down who you prayed for and what you prayed about.

my daughter to grow up healthy + thanked him for the miracle. Brent to find a job. Me + the gals w/ bible study. My mom + dad to keep working on their relationship. Kelsey to grow up to a young lady & find Christ. Brooke and Dan that their marriage is ok & God will help them, they are heavy on my heart. My dad & s-mom that they stay healthy & continue to heal. For my two friends that have babies! God always makes me think of other people & their needs, making me realize how blessed I am.

DAY 7: A WEEK IN REVIEW

Today take a few minutes to reflect on this week with your family.

1. What was the most enjoyable task you completed this week and why did you enjoy it so much?

   The hero story, because I have a hero of my own. And I love hearing/reading stories like that, melts my heart.

2. Which task did you find the most challenging and why?

   To write the letter, I haven't had time!... The hardest part for me is time management!

3. Which task made the most difference? Explain.

   Sitting without out anything around

focusing on God. Made me realize there are so many things to pray for! I don't do it enough.

4. Which task do you think made Jesus smile the most? Was there a moment this week that may have broken Jesus's heart?

- He would have smiled at the 20 min. task.
- Not giving him enough time!

5. What could be added to this week to make it even better?

Call a friend or family member you haven't spoke w/ in a while & let them know how wonderful they are.

WEEK 3: IT'S A BEAUTIFUL DAY IN THE NEIGHBORHOOD

Why is God's second greatest commandment so hard for so many people? This week we will tackle this quandary. I guarantee that you'll be outside of your comfort zone, which is where God usually resides. This week, you will need to focus on living out the following scripture:

> "Of all the commandments, which is the most important?"
>
> "The most important one," answered Jesus, "is this: hear, O Israel, the Lord our God, the Lord is one. Love the Lord your God with all your heart and with all your soul and with all your mind and with all your strength. The second is this: Love your neighbor as yourself. There is no commandment greater than these."
>
> Mark 12:28b-31

DAY 1: A CATCHPHRASE YOU CAN LIVE BY

Read each of the following adages. After careful consideration, answer the corresponding questions.

† Good fences make good neighbors.

_____

_____

† Your neighbor is the man who needs you.

_____

_____

† The fence that makes good neighbors needs a gate to make good friends.

_____

_____

1. Which phrase matches up with your relationship to your neighbors?

   Your neighbor is the man who needs you!

2. Provide your definition of "neighbor."

   Next door, friends, family, Christians.

DAY 2: GOOD BRIDGES MAKE GODLY NEIGHBORS

Jesus used parables to teach moral lessons, or as my pastor always says, "They are earthly stories with heavenly meanings." Motivational speaker Daniel Janssen shared the following anecdotal story with one of his audiences and has since published it on his website: www.danieljanssen.com. (Janssen 2012)

BUILDING BRIDGES WITH YOUR NEIGHBOR

A farmer had an argument with his neighbor over a wandering cow. When the disagreement ended, both were so angry they were willing to terminate their friendship. One day a traveling carpenter came to the farmer's house asking for work. After thinking about it for a bit the farmer said "yes."

He took the carpenter over to a stream and said "See that stream, it used to be a pond that my neighbor and I used to share, but we had an argument and my neighbor took his tractor and plowed a ditch so that the water flows between our properties separating us. I want you to build a fence along my property high enough that I don't have to see him anymore." The farmer left for town and the carpenter got to work. At the end of the day the farmer returned home with great expectations, hoping that a shiny new fence would stand between him and his disgruntled neighbor.

When the farmer drove up, he could see the carpenter, but did not see his fence. The farmer asked, "What have you been doing all day and where is my fence?" The carpenter took the farmer down to the stream and to the farmer's astonishment; he saw that a bridge stood between he and his neighbor's property. Before he could say anything, he saw his neighbor coming towards them. Within a few moments the neighbor had crossed the bridge coming up to the farmer saying "you are too good."

They mended their differences and rekindled the friendship. Later that evening the farmer asked the carpenter to stay on full time. He would give him full time work and pay him well. The carpenter declined saying, "I must go. There are more bridges to be built."

1. What are the two main lessons from this story?
   To love thy neighbor always + to always help head.

2. Do you have any relationships that need to be "bridged?" If so, what relationships are they? How do you plan on making that connection?

   Not that I am aware of, relationships weigh heavy on my heart!

DAY 3: CARPENTRY 101

As Richard C. Cushing once said, "Always plan ahead. It wasn't raining when Noah built the ark." Before you can begin to construct your bridge, you must first decide where your bridge needs to be built, develop a blueprint, and collect all the materials and tools you may need. I feel the need to forewarn you, this might be the first day that you begin to hesitate or struggle with this challenge. The first two weeks were all about you and your family, and for most of us, that is a comfortable place of solace. But from this day forward, there is no promise of an easy road. The great news is that whenever you feel unsure or scared, Jesus is walking right beside you, ready to give you a strength and courage you never knew you had.

1. You must first decide where your bridge should be placed. You may choose to rebuild a relationship or formulate a new relationship. In the space provided, describe where you're going to put your bridge and why you think this is the best place.

   _____
   _____
   _____

2. Do you have any reservations about this task? If so, write them in the space below.

3. What is God's purpose in (re)building this relationship?

DAY 4: THE GREAT CARPENTER

Today, you need to set aside time to read Mark 6:1-6. Consider the following questions as you read.

1. Why do you think that the people of His hometown were surprised that Jesus had so many followers?

___

2. What can we learn from Jesus's response to these people?

___

3. Although there are few other references to Jesus as a carpenter, no one denies that He is the Great Carpenter. List the ways in which He has helped build your life.

_____

_____

_____

_____

_____

_____

4. Can you think of any differences between those things constructed by Jesus and those constructed by the world?

_____

_____

_____

_____

_____

_____

5. In what way(s) can you improve your carpentry skills to be more Christlike?

_____

_____

_____

_____

_____

_____

DAY 5: SPENDING TIME WITH GOD

Today, take time to pray on the go. Put on your walking shoes and take a prayer walk around your neighborhood. Hopefully the weather will cooperate. Although you definitely don't want to seem like a stalker, please take a moment to pray for each of your neighbors as you pass their home. Also, if you see people out and about, take a minute to smile, wave, even strike up a conversation. In the space below, write about your experience. How did it go? Was it difficult? Did you have the opportunity to chat with anyone?

_____

_____

_____

_____

_____

_____

_____

_____

_____

_____

DAY 6: ROLLING UP YOUR SLEEVES

After prayerfully preparing for this day, you are ready to lay the foundation of your new bridge. Other than loving Jesus without limit, this is His second greatest request. Keep that in mind today as you wave goodbye to your safe and cozy bubble.

Look back at the plans you constructed on day three. It is time to (re)connect with whomever God has led you to contact.

DAY 7: A WEEK IN REVIEW

Take a few minutes to reflect on this week, especially yesterday's challenge.

1. What did you do to initiate (or renew) the relationship in your life?

   _____
   _____
   _____
   _____
   _____
   _____
   _____

2. How did the other person respond to your effort? Was their reaction what you thought it would be or somehow different than you expected?

   _____
   _____
   _____
   _____
   _____
   _____
   _____

3. Do you think God was pleased by your effort? Explain.

_____

_____

_____

_____

_____

_____

_____

4. Do you think you will ever attempt a task like this in the future? If not, what are your reservations?

_____

_____

_____

_____

_____

_____

_____

5. What did you learn about yourself and your relationship with God from this challenge?

_____

_____

_____

_____

_____

_____

_____

WEEK 4: BUILDING GOD'S HOUSE

It may be God's house, but is it the spiritual home? Many of us spend nearly every Sunday morning in a worship service. There is no doubt that fellowship and worship are main functions of any church. As the body of Christ, are you doing everything you can to support the mission of your church? After this week, hopefully you'll have a greater understanding of what Jesus intended the church to be and a more active role in pursuing this mission. After this week, you'll also be over halfway through the study! Keep up the good works!

DAY 1: ON A MISSION

Take a moment and consider the following questions.

1. What is your church's mission statement?

_____

_____

_____

_____

_____

_____

_____

2. List at least three activities that your church currently does to fulfill its mission.

†

†

†

3. To what extent have you participated in any of these activities?

_____

_____

_____

_____

_____

_____

_____

4. Are there any additional areas/activities that would further support the mission of your church?

_____

_____

_____

_____

_____

_____

_____

DAY 2: YOUR VERY OWN NICHE

Even if you are an identical twin, there is no one else in the world just like you. We all have our own talents, personality quirks, and abilities. This means that God created a niche for you that nobody else can truly fill. Please read the following scripture and consider what your niche might be.

> For by the grace given me I say to every one of you: Do not think of yourself more highly than you ought, but rather think of yourself with sober judgment, in accordance with the measure of faith God has given you. Just as each of us has one body with many members, and these members do not all have the same function, so in Christ we who are many form one body, and each member belongs to all the others. We have different gifts, according to the grace given us. If a man's gift is prophesying, let him use it in proportion to his faith. If it is serving, let him serve; if it is teaching, let him teach; if it is encouraging, let him encourage; if it is contributing to the needs of others, let him give generously; if it is leadership, let him govern diligently; if it is showing mercy, let him do it cheerfully.
>
> Romans 12:3-8

Using the remaining space, list some of your unique attributes and potential ways that God can use your abilities or weaknesses to become more active as the body of Christ.

DAY 3: THANK GOD FOR DIVERSITY

How dull would our day-to-day lives be if everyone was the same? If we looked the same, talked the same, dressed the same, acted the same, etc. Yawn. How merciful was God for providing diversity and variety? Beyond making our daily lives more interesting, diversity is essential to having a fully operational body of Christ.

Please read 1 Corinthians 12:12-27 and consider the following questions.

1. What excuse, if any, have you used to justify sitting on the sidelines in your church?

_____

_____

_____

_____

_____

_____

_____

2. Which verse did you find the most meaningful? Explain.

_____
_____
_____
_____
_____
_____
_____

3. After considering what you read yesterday and today, does this alter the way you perceive your role in your church? If so, how?

_____
_____
_____
_____
_____
_____
_____

DAY 4:
AFTER PRAYERFUL CONSIDERATION

"And let us consider how we may spur one another on toward love and good deeds" (Hebrews 10:24).

This week's prayer time is going to be a little different. You're going to make a collage. You can either use paper and scissors or you could make a digital collage by cutting and pasting from the web. You'll want to include anything that inspires your faith, both praise and prayer. Photos, quotes, lyrics, and whatever else fosters or inspires your communication with God. I included a picture of the *Prince of Peace* painted by eight year old, Akiane Kramarik, a photo of my son, a photo of the little girl I sponsor from Tanzania, Queen, and some of my favorite song lyrics, among other things.

_____
_____
_____
_____
_____
_____
_____

DAY 5: DECISIONS, DECISIONS

There is little more detrimental to the Christian faith than hearing a sermon on Sunday and doing nothing about it. As a member of the body, it's finally time to decide if and how you will choose to assist your church. Please don't feel confined to the brief period of this week or even this seven-week study when making your decision. Using the prompts below, consider how you will execute God's plan for you. It could be as simple as being a greeter or as involved as organizing a mission trip. As a member of the body of Christ, every volunteer is a missionary.

1. What action do you plan on taking?

_____

_____

_____

_____

_____

_____

_____

2. How much time do you anticipate devoting to this task (per week/month/year)?

_____

_____

_____

_____

_____

_____

_____

3. Who will you need to contact in order to begin?

_____

_____

_____

_____

_____

_____

_____

4. When will you start?

_____

_____

_____

_____

_____

_____

_____

DAY 6: MAKE THE CALL

Today all of your prayerful planning will finally pay off. It's time to turn those ideas into a reality. You should take the time to call someone at your church and let them know that you want to help and how. This was the day that I called our Connections Pastor, Tim Jones, to tell him about my LYFE work and explore the opportunity of leading a group through this study. I remember being really nervous because I seldom engage in a real conversation with my pastor. But he eased my anxiety and has been very encouraging throughout this process. It is just a reminder that *my fear* was no longer restraining my walk with Christ. Below are some points you may want to discuss with your church leader.

1. How you hope to get involved within and through the church.

_____
_____
_____
_____
_____
_____
_____

2. Why you feel compelled to help.

_____
_____
_____
_____
_____
_____

3. If they have any advice that will assist you in your effort.

_____
_____
_____
_____
_____
_____

4. If there anyone else at the church that you should contact.

_____
_____
_____
_____
_____
_____
_____

DAY 7: A WEEK IN REVIEW

Take a few minutes to reflect on this week, especially your new undertaking in God's house.

1. Was there any time during this week's study that made you uncomfortable? If so, why?

_____

_____

_____

_____

_____

_____

2. Do you plan on continuing your efforts in your church? Why or why not?

_____

_____

_____

_____

_____

_____

3. Is there a way that you could encourage others to faithfully participate as the body of Christ toward the mission of your church?

_____
_____
_____
_____
_____
_____
_____

Please do not leave this day's lesson without filling out the next sheet.

LYFE SUPPORT

I encourage you to find at least one partner for Week 5. Make sure that you know your partner's contact information and have discussed the following questions:

1. Who is/are your partner(s)?

_____

2. What is their e-mail address and phone number?

_____

_____

_____

_____

3. Are there any community service agencies or causes that you are already interested in working for/with? If so, please list them.

_____

_____

_____

_____

4. Is there a day of the week that is better for you to set aside several hours of time to donate to this community service mission?

_____

_____

_____

_____

You will need to be prayerful about what direction God wants you to take for this community service mission.

Rachel Kirkpatrick

WEEK 5: THE LEAST OF THESE

This week you will be spreading your wings a bit and getting out into the community. As you undoubtedly know, Jesus devoted His life to helping those in need. The blind, the lame, the judged, the diseased, and the deceased all found miracles through Jesus. Thank God, the Great Physician has saved all of our lives! Although we may not be doctors or miracle workers, we are lovers of Christ, and He has charged us with being His presence here on earth. Let us discover the biblical encouragement that will help us ready for our community service this week.

DAY 1: SCRIPTURAL COMPASS

Read the two passages below. Consider the question that follows.

> Therefore I urge you brothers, in view of God's mercy, to offer your bodies as living sacrifices, holy and pleasing to God—this is your spiritual act of worship. Do not conform any longer to the pattern of this world, but be transformed by the renewing of your mind. Then you will be able to test and approve what God's will is—his good, pleasing and perfect will.
>
> Romans 12:1-2

> In reply Jesus said: "A man was going down from Jerusalem to Jericho, when he fell into the hands of robbers. They stripped him of his clothes, beat him and went away, leaving him half dead. A priest happened to be going down the same road, and when he saw the man, he passed by on the other side. But a Samaritan, as he traveled, came where the man was; and when he saw him, he took pity on him. He went to him and bandaged his wounds, pouring on oil and wine. Then he put the man on his own donkey, took him to an inn and took care of him. The next day he took out two

silver coins and gave them to the innkeeper. 'Look after him,' he said, 'and when I return, I will reimburse you for any extra expense you may have.'"

Luke 10:30-35

1. Why do you think the priest ignored the man in need?

_____

_____

_____

_____

_____

2. Have you ever been in position to help someone, but "passed by on the other side"? If so, please explain.

_____

_____

_____

_____

_____

DAY 2: FINDING YOUR INNER MOTHER TERESA

Let's face it; we are not all Mother Teresa. She lived a self-sacrificial life in Calcutta, providing help to the helpless in India. Her work has now spread to over one hundred countries. She was just one woman who lived by Christ's example and made a difference in the lives she touched. You don't have to go to India, Africa, or Central America to find people in need of a helping hand and starving for salvation. You can make a difference right in your own community. According to motherteresa.org (Teresa 2012), one of Mother Teresa's favorite prayers was:

> Make us worthy, Lord, to serve our fellow man throughout the world who live and die in poverty and hunger. Give them, through our hands, this day their daily bread and, by our understanding love, give peace and joy.
>
> Mother Teresa

The challenge today is to write a short prayer at the bottom of this page that will embody your desire to help those in need. The greater feat will be continuing to include this in your prayer life beyond today, this week, and this study.

DAY 3: "SEEK AND YE SHALL FIND."
[MATTHEW 7:7]

One of the most common excuses I used or I have heard other Christians use to avoid volunteering is, "It's just not my calling." This is simply a copout. The Bible is very clear about the Christian obligation to take care of those who cannot take care of themselves. We have been entrusted to tend to widows, orphans, and homeless, among others. Moreover, God has given you a gift that will help you meet their needs.

The group of women who went through this study with me started two new mission projects. The first was Water Outreach. On Friday afternoons during the sweltering heat of July and August, we loaded ice-cold coolers of bottled water and oodles of crackers down to the local homeless shelter, KARM. We talked with people, prayed with people, and heard some fascinating stories. One of the most memorable people we met was Scrappy. For over twenty years, Scrappy was hooked on drugs and was homeless. In fact, he got his name because his "hustle" (as he called it) was that he found scrap metal and hawked it for spare money. However, when I met Scrappy, he was an employee of KARM with the keys and ID badge to prove it. He testified that his turnaround was due, in part, to faithful people who reached out and showed him Jesus' love. He now tries to be the loving, inspirational person that Jesus wants him to be.

The other mission project was PB & J (a.k.a. Peanut Butter and Jesus). Like many people, Kelly had this charitable project floating around in her head for some time. Through the prompting of this study and the encouragement from others in the group, Kelly organized a peanut butter drive and affixed various biblical versus to the jars to be handed out at the local food pantries. The first drive raised several hundred jars of peanut butter, which was able to help feed some very hungry and very appreciative people.

There are tons of examples of how Christians have used their talents to meet the needs of people. In my research for creative ways to serve, I ran across some interesting and amazing examples of people serving others based on their talents. After reading through the list, please take the time to discuss with your partner(s) how you can use your strengths to serve others.

- There is a Karaoke Coffee Club in L.A. that organizes a karaoke night for the homeless every Wednesday in downtown L.A. For a few hours each week, attendees are able to let go of their troubles and find joy in each other through fellowship and song.

For more inspiration or details about this group, you can visit www.homelesskaraoke.com.

- A group of college men at Eureka College started a mission project called, "Bearded Men Knitting Hats." You read that correctly. Yes, college men, with beards, learned how to knit and started selling their hats to raise money for a local women's shelter. How awesome is that?

- Dosomething.org is also an interesting resource for out-of-the-box ways to serve. There was even a man named Terrell, whose brother is an amputee. He is creating a system for amputees to buy, trade, or sell single shoes they're not using. I love it when God turns what we may think is a weakness into a strength!

DAY 4: SPICE IT UP

Today, take time to read the following scriptures and consider how God is calling you to be the salt and light in your community.

Matthew 25:34-45

_____

_____

_____

_____

Matthew 5:13-16

_____

_____

_____

_____

1. What do the previous scriptures suggest about our call to serve others?

_____

_____

_____

2. List at least three reasons why you think it is important for Christians to live a life of service.

   1. _____

   2. _____

   3. _____

3. What are some potential challenges or struggles in living a service life?

   _____
   _____
   _____
   _____
   _____

DAY 5: SPENDING TIME WITH GOD

"Humble yourselves, therefore, under God's mighty hand, that he may lift you up in due time. Cast all your anxiety on him because he cares for you." 1 Peter 5:6-7

Today take the time to rewrite this verse into your own personal prayer. Be specific about your worries and why you trust Him to bring resolution.

_____
_____
_____
_____
_____
_____
_____
_____
_____
_____
_____
_____
_____
_____

DAY 6: WHISTLE WHILE YOU WORK

Today is the day you and your partner start helping within the community. Please be aware that you are doing more than just physically assisting others—you may be the first person who has ever attempted to show someone Jesus's love. It's not necessary to show up with a sermon ready to go; simply show kindness, compassion, and love. When the opportunity presents itself, share your passion for Jesus.

DAY 7: A WEEK IN REVIEW

Today take a few minutes to reflect on this week. Please be candid about your experience working with the needy.

1. Which scripture from this week inspired or comforted you the most? Explain.

   _____

   _____

   _____

   _____

   _____

   _____

2. Where did you end up serving and what kind of work did you do?

   _____

   _____

   _____

   _____

   _____

   _____

3. Who was the most memorable person you met and why?

_____

_____

_____

_____

_____

_____

4. Did you get a chance to be Jesus to someone? If so, please share your story.

_____

_____

_____

_____

_____

_____

5. Do you plan on continuing your work? Explain.

_____

_____

_____

6. What did you learn about yourself and your relationship with God this week?

WEEK 6:
GIVE AND YOU SHALL BELIEVE

For some of us, giving is much easier than receiving. If you agree with this statement, then this week is going to be such a gift for you. If you recall in Week 1, you were challenged to start setting aside all your spare cash. Hopefully you met your goal and have considered the sacrifices along the way as small gestures of devotion to Christ. This week you will really think about your definition of wealth and how you exercise faith within your financial life.

DAY 1: MONEY IS THE ROOT OF ALL CLICHÉS?

Please fill in the blanks below.

† "_____ can't buy you happiness."

† "Put your _____ where your mouth is."

† "Time is _____."

† "_____ doesn't grow on trees."

These are only a few of the plethora of clichés about money. Americans are bombarded every day with advertising, media, and peer pressure to make, spend, and invest their money. Maybe this week will provide some refreshing clarity about your wealth, where it comes from, and what to do with at least some of it.

The pastor at my church, G. W. Boles, made a statement one Sunday that still echoes through my memory. He said, "Christians are [spiritual] millionaires, but most of them live in [spiritual] poverty because they don't even know what they have." My close friend, Angelina, recently returned from a mission trip to Haiti. I was struck by her comment that she admired Haitian faith. She said that they have a degree of faith she'd never witnessed before. In all of their poverty, their faith is all many of them have. Most Americans are so surrounded by creature comforts (home, food, clean water…) that our faith is muted because we don't *have to* rely on the Lord to meet our basic needs. I admit that I sometimes forget what a blessed life I've been given. Let this week remind us that we are nothing and have nothing without God.

"But remember the Lord your God, for it is he who gives you the ability to produce wealth, and so confirms his covenant, which he swore to your forefathers, as it is today" (Deuteronomy 8:18).

DAY 2: YOU CAN'T TAKE IT WITH YOU

It's true; all the money in the world won't get you any closer to heaven. In fact, Scripture is clear about the dangers of greed and money worship. Please read the scriptures listed below and complete the tasks that follow.

Matthew 19: 23-24

Why do you think this statement is true?

_____

_____

_____

_____

Ecclesiastes 5:10-15

Can you think of any examples, either personal or from the media, that demonstrate the truth of this passage?

_____

_____

_____

_____

1 Timothy 6:7-10

Have you ever loved money or material wealth? If so, please elaborate on what your motivation may have been.

___

American culture seems to celebrate wealth. Do you think you participate in this celebration? Explain.

___

Do you think there is a difference between greed and wanting to be wealthy? If so, explain.

___

DAY 3: ALL THE RIGHT REASONS

"Give cheerfully." Our worship leader at church reminds us of this before the tithes and offerings are taken up each Sunday. Tithing at church or donating to charity may feel like just another bill to pay. However, God is more concerned about a generous heart than a big, obligatory check.

Please read the two passages listed below and summarize them in your own words. While you're reading, ask yourself: what does God want you to understand about charity?

2 Corinthians 8:1-15

_____

_____

_____

2 Corinthians 9:6-15

_____

_____

_____

DAY 4: THE PRAYOFF

"Be joyful always; pray continually; give thanks in all circumstances, for this is God's will for you in Christ Jesus" (Thessalonians 5:16-18).

Ann Voskamp, author of *One Thousand Gifts*, challenges herself and her readers to acknowledge God's constant presence by thanking Him for all the blessings He bestows on us each day (Voskamp 2010). She writes, "The holy grail of joy is not in some exotic location or some emotional mountain peak experience. The joy of wonder could be here! Here, in the messy, piercing ache of now, joy might be—unbelievably—possible! The only place we need to see before we die is this place of seeing God, here and now." Today set aside at least twenty minutes in praise. Make a list of all the ways God has blessed you, for which you are thankful.

_____

_____

_____

_____

_____

_____

DAY 5: THE RICH FAMILY AT CHURCH

Read the following short story by Eddie Ogan from www.omegatimes.com. (Ogan 2012)

THE RICHEST FAMILY IN OUR CHURCH

I'll never forget Easter 1946. I was 14, my little sister Ocy was 12, and my older sister Darlene 16. We lived at home with our mother, and the four of us knew what it was to do without many things. My dad had died five years before, leaving Mom with seven school kids to raise and no money.

By 1946 my older sisters were married and my brothers had left home. A month before Easter the pastor of our church announced that a special Easter offering would be taken to help a poor family. He asked everyone to save and give sacrificially. When we got home, we talked about what we could do. We decided to buy 50 pounds of potatoes and live on them for a month. This would allow us to save $20 of our grocery money for the offering. Then we thought that if we kept our electric lights turned out as much as possible and didn't listen to the radio we'd save money on that month's electric bill. Darlene got as many house and yard cleaning jobs as possible, and both of us babysat for everyone we could. For 15 cents we could buy enough cotton loops to make three potholders to sell for $1. We made $20 on potholders.

That month was one of the best of our lives. Every day we counted the money to see how much we had saved. At night we'd sit in the dark and talk about how the poor family was going to enjoy having the money the church would give them. We had about 80 people in church, so we figured that whatever amount of money we had to give, the offering would surely be 20 times that much. After all, every Sunday the pastor had reminded everyone to save for the sacrificial offering.

The day before Easter, Ocy and I walked to the grocery store and got the manager to give us three crisp $20 bills and one $10 bill for all our change. We ran all the way home to show Mom and Darlene. We had never had so much money before. That night we were so excited we could hardly sleep. We didn't care that we wouldn't have new clothes for Easter; we had $70 for the sacrificial offering. We could hardly wait to get to church!

On Sunday morning, rain was pouring. We didn't own an umbrella, and the church was a mile from our home, but it did not matter how wet we got. Darlene had cardboard in her shoes to fill the holes. The cardboard came apart and her feet got wet. But we sat in church proudly. I heard some teenagers talking about the Smith girls having on their old dresses. I looked at them in their new clothes and I felt rich.

When the sacrificial offering was taken, we were sitting on the second row from the front. Mom put in the $10 bill, and each of us kids put in $20. As we walked home after church we sang all the way. At lunch Mom had a surprise for us. She had bought a dozen eggs and we had boiled Easter eggs with our fried potatoes! Late that afternoon the minister drove up in his car. Mom went to door, talked with him for a moment, and then came back with an envelope in her hand. We asked what it was, but she didn't say a word. She opened the envelope, and out fell a bunch of money. There were three crisp $20 bills, one $10 and seventeen $1 bil!s. Mom put the money back in the envelope. We didn't talk, just sat and stared at the floor. We had gone from feeling like millionaires to feeling like poor white trash. We kids had such a happy life that we felt sorry for anyone who didn't have our Mom and Dad for parents and a house full of brothers and sisters and other kids visiting constantly. We thought it was fun to share silverware and see whether we got the spoon or the fork that night. We had two knives that we passed around to whoever needed them. I knew we didn't have a lot of things that other people had, but I'd never thought we were poor. I didn't like being poor. I looked at my dress and worn-out shoes and felt so ashamed—I didn't even want to go back to church. Everyone there probably already knew we were poor! I thought about school. I was in the ninth grade and at the top of my class of over 100 students. I wondered if the kids at school knew that we were poor. I decided that I could quit school since I had finished the eighth grade. That was all the law required at that time. We sat in silence for a long time. Then it got dark, and we went to bed. All that week we girls went to school and came home, and no one talked much.

Finally on Saturday, Mom asked us what we wanted to do with the money. What did poor people do with money? We didn't know. We'd never known we were poor. We didn't want to go to church on Sunday, but Mom said we had to. Although it was a sunny day, we didn't talk on the way. Mom started to sing, but no one joined in and she only sang one verse. At church we had a missionary speaker. He talked about how churches in Africa made buildings out of sun dried bricks, but they needed money to buy roofs. He said $100 would put a roof on a church. The minister said, "Can't we all sacrifice to help these poor people?" We looked at each other and smiled for the first time in a week. Mom reached into her purse and pulled out the envelope. She passed it to Darlene. Darlene gave it to me, and I handed it to Ocy. Ocy put it in the offering. When the offering was counted, the minister announced that it was a little over $100. The missionary was excited. He hadn't expected such a large offering from our small church. He said, "You must have some rich people in this church." Suddenly it struck us! We had given $87 of that "little over $100." We were the rich family in the church! Hadn't the missionary said so? From that day on I've never been poor again.

According to this demonstration of spiritual wealth, do you consider your family, church, and country "wealthy"? Explain.

_____

_____

_____

_____

_____

_____

DAY 6: "SHOW ME THE MONEY!"

You've researched a great cause, you've saved your spare cash, and today you finally get to let it go. Please remember that it's not just money that you're parting with; it's the worldly view of wealth that you're parting with too. Give with humility and cheer knowing that your sacrifice was worth the blessings your gift will provide.

DAY 7: A WEEK IN REVIEW

1. Where/who did you donate your money to?

___

2. How did you deliver the money?

___

3. If you know, how will your donation be used?

___

4. How did you feel when you let it go?

5. Has your view on worldly wealth changed at all? If so, how?

6. Beyond tithing, are you willing to make more monetary contributions in the future? Explain.

7. Do you think that sacrificing personal comfort is necessary to truly give in a godly way?

_____

_____

_____

_____

_____

WEEK 7: WRAPPING IT UP

Hopefully over the past six weeks you have strengthened your faith and (re)discovered your passion for Christ. Undoubtedly, some weeks were harder than others. This week you'll get the chance to really digest your spiritual journey throughout this study.

DAY 1: A WORD FROM GOD

I've yet to meet a Christian who has actually heard God's omnipotent voice beckoning from the sky. The good news is that we can hear His message every day by perusing through His Word. Every week of this study, you were given scripture to read and think about. Take some time to review all of the passages you read during this study. After thoughtful consideration, answer the following questions.

Romans 12:1-2, 3-8	James 1:14-26	Philippians 4:6-7
Mark 10:29-31	Mark 12:28-31	Mark 6:1-6
1 Corinthians 12:12-27	Hebrews 10:24	Proverbs 1:5
Luke 10:30-35	Deuteronomy 8:18	1 Timothy 6:7-10
Matthew 5:13-16	Matthew 25:34-45	Matthew 19:23-4
Ecclesiastes 5:10-15	1 Thessalonians 5:16-18	1 Peter 5:6-7
2 Corinthians 8:1-15	2 Corinthians 9:12-15	

1. Which scriptures or stories were you already familiar with?

_____

_____

_____

2. Were there any verses that you discovered for the first time, or found new meaning from during this study? If so, which one(s) and why?

DAY 2: WEAKEST WEEK

Week 1: Growing from the Inside Out
Week 2: Putting Family First
Week 3: It's a Beautiful Day in the Neighborhood
Week 4: Building God's House
Week 5: The Least of These
Week 6: Give and You Shall Believe

You have devoted countless hours over the past six weeks in prayer, reading Scripture, and donating your time, energy, and resources so that you could live more Christlike. Can you imagine living this way every day for the rest of your life? Jesus did. Reflect back on each week's task and consider the following questions.

1. Which activity was the most meaningful and why?

_____

_____

_____

_____

_____

_____

_____

2. Which week was the greatest struggle for you? Explain.

_____
_____
_____
_____
_____
_____
_____

3. Did you have any moments where you knew God was with you or encouraging you? If so, when and what happened?

_____
_____
_____
_____
_____
_____
_____

DAY 3: ALL WE NEED IS LOVE

An abundance of themes are woven throughout the New Testament, including atonement, forgiveness, compassion, and certainly love. Hopefully during your journey through this study you have rekindled your love or, better yet, passion for Christ. However, all our adoration for Christ pales in comparison to His love for us. Please read the following scripture and reflect on how this study helped you realize the merits of this passage.

> Whoever does not love does not know God, because God is love. This is how God showed his love among us: He sent his one and only Son into the world that we might live through him. This is love: not that we loved God, but that he loved us and sent his Son as an atoning sacrifice for our sins. Dear friends, since God so loved us, we also ought to love one another. No one has ever seen God; but if we love one another, God lives in us and his love is made complete in us.
>
> 1 John 4:8-12

 Rachel Kirkpatrick

1. Which task made you feel the closest to God? Explain.

2. As this study is coming to a close, do you feel closer to God? If so, how?

DAY 4: A CLOSING PRAYER

Dear Father,

Thank you so much for holding our hands throughout this journey. Lord, thank you for the faithful and fearless followers you led to and through the LYFE study. Thank you for the bridges that were built in your great name. Lord, where we tossed out our pebbles of faith and compassion, let those demonstrations of your love and worthiness ripple indefinitely through the world. I pray for continued selflessness in the name of Jesus for all of your children. Our small sacrifices are but a token for the debt we owe you, but in our gratitude, may we always be willing to sacrifice our comforts (money, time, expectations, and routines) to demonstrate what is possible in your name. Lord, thank you for all of my weaknesses and flaws. I now know they are my greatest strengths because that is when I'm relying on you the most. Lord, please remind us, when we face our Goliaths, that you will always give us everything we need to overcome our fears. Thank you, Lord, for your abundance. Thank you for showing us The Way. May our lives in this world bring a glimpse of the hereafter to those who haven't met you yet. We are awestruck and humbled by your greatness.

Your loving daughter,

Rachel

DAY 5: "BE THE CHANGE YOU WISH TO SEE IN THE WORLD." [MAHATMA GANDHI]

You may remember that on Day 1 of the first week of this study you were asked to do some self-reflection. Please reconsider the questions posed on Day 1, the answers you gave, and how (if at all) your answers have changed.

Please answer all of the following questions again having completed six weeks of this study.

1. Besides Jesus, who do you admire the most and why?

_____

_____

_____

_____

2. What is the hardest thing for you to give up in order for you to be more obedient to Him?

_____

_____

_____

_____

3. What is your favorite part about being a Christian?

___

4. What is your least favorite part about being a Christian?

___

5. List at least three things you got out of this study.

†

†

†

6. How will this study impact your future?

___

DAY 6: CARE TO SHARE?

You have already given your time, energy, and resources. Now comes the easy part: you need to find three people to share your experience with. This is not an opportunity to be boastful of your accomplishments; it is a time to share in your amazing journey with Christ. Please keep the following scripture in mind when you are sharing your experience.

> Are we beginning to commend ourselves again? Or do we need, like some people, letters of recommendation to you or from you? You yourselves are our letter, written on our hearts, known and read by everybody. You show that you are a letter from Christ, the result of our ministry, written not with ink but with the Spirit of the living God, not on the tablets of stone but on tablets of human hearts.
>
> Such confidence as this is ours through Christ before God. Not that we are competent in ourselves to claim anything for ourselves, but our competence comes from God. He has made us competent as ministers of a new covenant—not of the letter but of the Spirit; for the letter kills, but the Spirit gives life.
>
> 2 Corinthians 3:1-6

1. Who did you tell?

_____
_____
_____

2. What were their responses?

_____
_____
_____
_____
_____
_____
_____
_____
_____

DAY 7: ONLY THE BEGINNING

If nothing else, this study challenged me to remember Jesus just as much Monday through Saturday as on Sunday. My LYFE adventure allowed me to meet and work with some pretty incredible people. The most impressive person I had the opportunity to talk with was Eddie Ogan, author of *The Rich Family in Church*. I wanted to make sure I could use her story in the study. After some crafty use of the internet, I tracked down her phone number in Washington State. I started to get nervous as I dialed the long-distance number. I had sweaty palms, my heart was racing, and I wondered what I was going to say. After a few rings, the sage voice of an eighty-year-old woman was on the other end. I made sure I'd dialed the correct number and then quickly said, "My name is Rachel Kirkpatrick. I'm not selling anything so please don't hang up the phone." She was so kind, especially considering I was a complete stranger who lived on the other side of the country. I told her about myself and my LYFE experience. I quickly realized she is the embodiment of LYFE.

Eddie's story wasn't a story at all; it was about her life. She had written the story down in one of her monthly letters she sends to missionaries from her church. It inspired the missionaries so much that they posted her story on the web and that's how I found it.

We talked for about an hour about our lives. I learned that she and her husband had thirteen children, twelve of whom were adopted. In addition, they fostered seventy-seven children over the past several decades. I commented that it must have taken a fortune to raise all those kids. Without hesitating, she said they always knew that God would give them everything they needed.

I imagined her home as warm and inviting with afghans and quilts over the backs of chairs and couches. I wondered if her kitchen always smelled of cookies and I knew, beyond a doubt, that she gives great hugs. In our brief conversation, I realized that she might be the richest person I'd ever met. And hopefully one day, if I stay faithful, I will be a spiritual millionaire too. Maybe we can all discover God's riches in our lives and continue to put our faith into action, in spite of the cost. We can't all move to Africa, adopt twelve children, or write studies, but we can follow Him. I heard a Jill Phillips song that said, "You don't have to save the world; all you have to do is show up." Just show up each day ready to be His hands and feet. Love yourself as He loves you. Cherish and nurture your family, neighbors, church, and community as He does. Remember that wealth is measured less by your bank account than by your perception of true riches. As the newness of this study wears off, which it always does, ask yourself this question: What are you doing to shine light in the darkness and live your faith every day?

NOTES

Dr. Wayne W. Dyer, *The Power of Intention* (New York: Hay House Inc., 2010), 45-47.

Daniel Janssen. www.danieljanssen.com (accessed January 30, 2012).

Mother Teresa. motherteresa.org (accessed January 30, 2012).

Ann Voskamp. *One Thousand Gifts: A Dare to Live Fully Right Where You Are* (Grand Rapids: Zondervan, 2010), 33.

Eddie Ogan. www.omegatimes.com (accessed January 30, 2012).